Norse Stories

Retold by Robert Hull
Illustrated by Adam Stower
and Jonathon Heap

Thomson Learning

New York

Tales from Around the World

African Stories
Egyptian Stories
Greek Stories
Native North American Stories
Norse Stories
Roman Stories

Editor: Katie Roden
Series Designer: Tracy Gross
Book Designer: Mark Whitchurch
Color artwork by Adam Stower
Black and white artwork by Jonathon Heap
Map on page 48 by Peter Bull
Consultant: Dr. Andy Orchard,
Emmanuel College, Cambridge, England

First published in the
United States in 1993 by
Thomson Learning
115 Fifth Avenue
New York, NY 10003

First published in 1993 by
Wayland (Publishers) Ltd.

Library of Congress Cataloging-in-Publication Data
Hull, Robert, 1936-
  Norse Stories / retold by Robert Hull ; illustrated by Adam Stower and Jonathan Heap.
      p.   cm. – (Tales from around the world)
  Includes bibliographical references (p.).
  Contents: The beginning of things – Odin drinks wisdom – Gullweig the Golden – Giant-slaughtering – Balder's death – Ragnarok.
  ISBN 1-56847-131-9
  1. Mythology, Norse – Juvenile literature. I. Stower, Adam. II. Heap, Jonathon. III. Title.
IV. Series.
BL860.H855   1993
398.2'089'3 – dc20   93-30731

Printed in Italy

Contents

Introduction

*F*ire meeting ice. Red-hot lava and white-hot rock blasted out of the burning depths of the earth, to hiss down on dazzling ice and heaped snow.

That is what the Vikings, roving explorers from the Norse lands of Scandinavia, saw in Iceland, as mountains broke open and scattered fire on the glaciers and the snowbound earth. That frightening vision became the Vikings' story of how the world began.

They made stories from the things they saw. From the hot springs seething up out of the earth, with clouds of steam hanging over them, they made a story about a well of wisdom.

From the melting of icebergs and glaciers they made a tale of the first being. It took shape under the drip of thaw, as if it had been trapped, buried beneath the ice.

Perhaps the Viking storytellers remembered discovering an animal stored in ice in the winter's great deep freeze. Perhaps they remembered digging it out and taking food from its huge, frozen carcass.

The Vikings also brought a rich cargo of Norse stories with them from their homes in Norway, Sweden, and Denmark. They brought gods and goddesses. They brought loads of giants and trolls and elves and ogres, with a heap of names. They brought a magic gold ring that made more gold rings, an eight-legged horse faster than the wind, wolves that chased the sun and moon, dwarfs who hid from the light, and deep-sea dragons.

They brought a fabulous hoard of poems and songs. They hammered them out in the forges of their magic minds, shaping them from hard lives on the fjords and fells, from years of sea and snow and winds.

And perhaps they brought stories from farther away. Like Odin, their chief god, they traveled the world – for knowledge and stories. Long before Iceland became a Viking home in the ninth and tenth centuries, they had warred and traded all over Europe. They went to Kiev, to Baghdad, to Constantinople, to Pisa, to Seville. They colonized over half the islands of Britain. They settled in the Orkneys, and the Faroe Islands, halfway to Iceland.

Even after they had settled in Iceland, some of them went off to find the lands that are now called Greenland, Labrador, and Newfoundland, reaching North America five hundred years before Columbus. A restless people, hungry for things to happen.

It's no wonder the Vikings made up marvelous stories. They welled up clear and fresh from the wise minds of Vikings long gone; the Vikings who went to Iceland and have lived there as a nation ever since.

The Beginning of Things

Odin, the chief of the gods, called up Volva, the prophetess, from the depths of the world. He wanted to hear the story of the world. He wanted to know how it began, and how it would end.

Volva spoke.

"No soil, no sea, no sand, no wind, no waves, no light, no life.

"That was the beginning. Nothing. There was endless dark and emptiness, called Ginnungagap – Yawning Gap.

"Then worlds came into being. The first world was fire. In the south of Ginnungagap came burning and terrible light. That first world of flame, a world impossible to live in, was called Muspell.

"The second world was ice. In the north, at the bottom of Ginnungagap, a great well heaved and spat. Over its rim crawled poisonous rivers, which trailed out into the darkness. Huge winds whipped spray from them, which turned to drizzling rain and settled as frost, piling up into shelves of ice. The yeasty poison in the flowing waters thickened and congealed, and the rivers ground to a halt and they too became ice. That second world of ice, a world impossible to live in, was called Niflheim.

"Fire and ice. Furnace-heat and death-cold. Two worlds. Then, the sparks and embers hurled out of Muspell met the towering ice of Niflheim, and the air became warm, like a summer night. This was World.

"The first being came. This is how.

"Over ages of time, the ice grew to an immense height. In the warm air it creaked and swayed, and with a splintering yell a towering bulk of ice broke free on its own. That was the first being. He was Ymir, the Roarer. He founded the race of evil giants. This is how. He lay there. He slept, and sweat welled. The sweat ran onto the surrounding ice, and a thaw ran and dripped, and the ice groaned and cracked into more ice giants. From them, later, came the terrible families of frost ogres, the frost giants.

"These, Odin, were the first beings: Ymir the Roarer, and his evil race of ogres."

Odin knew all this. He knew the beginning of the story of the world, but he did not know the end. He knew also that Volva had to tell the story of the world from the beginning. Her story was one story. Odin waited. Would she say more now, or would the end remain unspoken?

She went on, "Other beings came. The gods came. This is how.

"The gods were buried in ice, waiting to live. The warmth of Muspell, meeting the cold of Niflheim, was like a great breath licking at the ice, uncovering what was lying there. The first being that was released from the ice was the first animal being, the cow called Authumla. Authumla licked at the ice for her food. Her licking uncovered another being, Buri, the first of the Aesir gods. All the gods were waiting, and were slowly released from their cells of deep ice, by being licked into their shapes by the warm breath of the world.

"Buri uncovered Borr, then Borr married a giant, Bestla. They had three sons, Vili, Ve, and – the greatest of the three – you, the Allfather, Odin. Then there were more gods, and you were all called the Aesir.

"Then the earth came. This is how.

"You remember, Odin, that you and your brothers Vili and Ve, the three Aesir gods, heard the fury of the ice giant Ymir, the Roarer, as he tramped and rampaged about the world, shattering whatever lay in his way. You knew that you would not be safe in the world if Ymir lived."

7

Odin wanted to know the future, not the past, but he could not interrupt Volva. If he did, she would fade back to the grave, her story unfinished. So Odin listened again to the great tale of his own greatest deeds, long ago when he slew Ymir and made the earth.

"You fought against Ymir, the ice giant. You dazzled him and hacked at him with a million swords of flame, till he retreated and sprawled lifeless, trickles of milky blood flowing from him. This icy, foaming, white blood became the sea. Then from Ymir's body you made earth, the world we call Midgard, which means the yard in the middle.

"Ymir's bones were the mountains. The dome of his skull became the curving sky. Then, to mark the victory, Odin, you planted the ash called Yggdrasil, the Tree of All the Worlds. It binds them together. Standing next to the house of earth, it holds the earth in place and keeps the sky up.

"That is why the tree of Yggdrasil spreads through all the worlds, holding them together. Its roots are in the depths of the worlds, its topmost leaves are beyond the stars. Its boughs are forever wet with white dews, and from them fall the floods of the world.

"So you, Odin, with the help of Vili and Ve, your brothers, first lifted up the world. You first made the land of men, the clearing called Midgard, the incomparable earth. The sun shone from the south on to the dry land and on the ground grew the soft grass.

"To the east you made a boundary for Jotunheim, the land of giants. In Midgard you built Asgard as a home for the gods. You placed a river, Ifing, between Jotunheim and Midgard. You built a bridge, Bifrost, reaching up to Asgard from Midgard. It is guarded by Heimdall, the god who can hear grass or the wool of sheep growing.

"From the south came the sun, and alongside her the moon. At first the sun rolled along the top of the land from west to east, not rising into the sky, not knowing what journey to take. The stars had no knowledge of where to stand, the moon of how to change.

10

"The Aesir gathered for a discussion and gave names to the night and the new moon. They gave names to the morning and midday, the afternoon and evening. They gave order to the year.

"The gods met again on the Shining Strand. They built altars of timber, and temples. They built forges to fashion metal. They made tongs and tools.

"The gods found gold. They made jewels and arm-rings. With gold disks they played games in the garth.

"Then there came people, the race of humans, to live in Midgard. This is how.

"To the coast came three of the gods – you, Odin, and your brothers, Vili and Ve. You found there, on the land, two fallen trees. You set them erect, and made of them Ask and Embla, the first people. Ask and Embla possessed no senses, or soul, or breath; but you, Odin, gave them a soul, and Vili gave them sight and hearing, and Ve breathed breath into them.

"But they would not be like the Aesir. This is why.

"Three young giant-women came from the east, the land of the giants. The three young giant-women, the Norns, had a terrible power. They sat under the spreading boughs of Yggdrasil, with pieces of wood in their hands. In the wood they carved the fates of all men and women. They notched the day of their birth. They chose what lives they would lead. They marked the moment of their deaths.

"That was how the worlds began. That is all the story I shall tell. To know how the worlds will end you must wait."

Volva fell silent and disappeared. Odin, first of the gods, most powerful of the gods, did not even know his own future.

Odin Drinks Wisdom

From his high throne in Asgard, Odin could *see* everywhere in the worlds.

Every eagle swooping over the fjord for fish, every seal basking on ice was visible to him. Each dawn he released his two ravens, called Hugin and Mugin, Thought and Memory. They flew from Asgard and roved the worlds, searching for things to know. Each evening they returned to Asgard, bringing home new truths to Odin.

Odin heard terrible prophecies. There would be war between the Aesir and another race. Many of the Aesir would die. They were doomed. He wanted to know the truth about these prophecies, and decided to travel the worlds himself.

Odin already had more knowledge of death than the living have. Long ago he had hung for nine nights and nine days on a branch of Yggdrasil until he was almost dead, and glimpsed in the distances of his mind some of the knowledge of those who have died.

Odin wrapped his cloak around him and went among the race of people, listening to stories and omens. None held the truth about the doom of the gods. He asked the first things. At the volcano's edge he peered into fire and listened to its restless voice, but there was no rumor in it about the future. He consulted ice. He stood close to the grinding skirmish of ice floes and tried to listen to them, but their voices were meaningless.

Odin changed his shape and became a seal. Swimming under the ice he heard the long songs of whales, echoing and echoing. He lay on beaches of snow and heard the fish-eagles scream, but not of the doom of the gods. He became an otter, and nosed up rivers to find the scent of death, traces of the future. But Odin could find nothing that confirmed the prophecies.

Finally he decided to ask Mimir. Mimir had great wisdom, which he drew from his own deep well. He guarded the well jealously, letting no other being drink from it. The wisdom-filled waters welled from under a root of Yggdrasil. One root began in Asgard, another in Midgard. Mimir's well was under the third root, the one that began in Jotunheim.

Odin walked down through the earth, following the winding trail of the root of Yggdrasil. When it turned in the direction of the land of the frost ogres and cliff giants, the path grew hard and cold under his feet. Odin saw mist hanging over the trail ahead of him. He walked on, and there came to his ears the slop and gulp of heaving water.

It was the well of Mimir. A seething pool of milky, white water was overhung by an icy rockface that the winds had carved into a wolfish snarl. On one side, curtains of greenish ice hung from the frozen rock. Behind them, Mimir was crouched over his source of power. He was gazing deep into it, waiting for the right time to drink.

Odin was cautious. He could not pretend, or take a different shape. Mimir would know him.

"Odin I am. I want to know the end. I want to know who will live, and who will die. Let me drink at your well of wisdom. Once. Once will tell me."

"Not once. Not without sacrifice. There is no drinking at the well of wisdom without sacrifice. Knowledge is power. Your drinking will draw off some of my power."

"What must I give as payment, in sacrifice? Let it be what you will."

"A seeing eye. For one drink, one eye."

Odin should have known. He had hung on the tree for nine days and nearly died. He had nearly given his last breath for knowledge. If he had to give half his seeing it did not surprise him.

"For a single drink, a single eye! So be it!" Odin tore an eye from his face and threw it into the waiting well. The seething water grew still.

Mimir handed Odin the Gjallarhorn, the crescent-shaped drinking horn. "Only from this must you drink."

Odin knelt, and scooped Gjallarhorn through the water. He rose to his feet, and took one long gulp. As he drank, something flashed into his mind, coursing through it like a stream in spate, or like the bounding aurora that rises tingling into the night sky. The well had told him, in one moment of racing truth, that there would be war between the Aesir and an older race of gods.

Odin handed Gjallarhorn back to Mimir. He looked into the well and met the unwavering gaze of his own eye from the well's depths. Staring back up at him, it seemed restless, moving to and fro in the swaying water.

In the darkness, on his way back to Asgard, Odin saw the moon reflected in a lake. Like an eye. Like an eye the sun gleamed on the ice at dawn. Like an eye the sun still gleamed when the clouds surrounded it.

There would be a war with the Vanir, the older gods. But was this to be the only war?

Odin had not been told the end of the story of the world. He only knew that somewhere a war waited to come into being.

15

Gullweig the Golden

Odin, the one-eyed god, had drunk wisdom at the well of Mimir. One drink from the Gjallarhorn had filled him with the knowledge that there would be a war with the Vanir, the older gods.

He had been told no more. His mind hurled questions back and forth in his skull. Was this the beginning of the end of the story of the world? Which gods would live? Who would die?

He knew that he must try to make peace with the Vanir, the gods of the shining spaces above Yggdrasil. The Vanir were mysterious gods of earlier times who were never seen in Asgard or Midgard. Their names, except for one or two, were unknown. Only a few had been heard of, like Niord, a great sea god, and Freya, a goddess of love and war.

Odin sent out his ravens. They cried toward the Vanir into the gleaming spaces above Yggdrasil, but there was no answer. They soared and circled, croaking, questioning the mountain summits and leaning snow-walls. Wings glinting in the low sun, they flew down over grinding ice-roads, up through heaving snow-mists. No voice rang in answer from the Vanir. The ravens heard only giant-clatter and the thunder and thump of traveling storm trolls and ice ogres.

The ravens returned, and Odin was no wiser. He was about to set out himself, when a giant-girl came to Asgard. She called herself Gullweig. Her eyes, hair, and skin shone like the gold of sunrise, and she moved among the Aesir like sunlight through mountains.

Odin was suspicious. Perhaps she had been sent from the Vanir. Could she be a Vanir witch-goddess? Or even Freya?

Gullweig joined the Aesir in the shade of Yggdrasil, where they were playing checkers with gold disks. One day she picked up a disk and gazed at it the way she might have gazed at her own child.

"Is there anything more beautiful than gold?" She smiled. And she kissed the gold disk.

Plain-thoughted Thor spoke. "A farm at first light is more beautiful than gold, or a ship's sails in the mist. Many ordinary things are far more beautiful."

Gullweig teased the good-hearted Thor. "I cannot wear ships' sails, or a farm at first light. A plain gold arm-ring or a beautifully made necklace would suit me much better, especially if a dwarf, deep underground, hammered it and set the jewels."

For several days Gullweig stayed with the gods, in the shade of Yggdrasil. Her talk of riches and beauty began to weary them. Then she crossed over the bridge Bifrost, and walked into Midgard to see men and women.

Gullweig stayed many months in Midgard. Odin watched her every move from his high throne, and his ravens gathered stories about her. He began to think she was not one of the Vanir. She must have come from Jotunheim, bringing great danger to the Aesir.

Wherever the beautiful Gullweig stayed in Midgard, it was as if the people were entranced by her. As they listened to her, their minds, like a fleet of ships coming about to face a new direction, turned toward gold. After a time, Odin saw that the people of Midgard were no longer happy. Golden-haired, golden-skinned Gullweig (if that *was* her name) had scattered into their hearts the terrible love of gold. They hid it in heaps in caves, they changed its beauty into money. Then came murder, lying, thieving, cheating – all for gold.

It seemed that the malice of the giants had sent lust for gold into the minds of men. Gullweig had come to make misery and trouble, and succeeded. It was a victory for evil, for the giants.

Then Gullweig came back to Asgard. She tried to repeat her victory among the Aesir. She spoke of her love of gold. She showed the gods her new necklace, Brisingamen, which she had been given by the dwarfs, she said. She did not reveal that the gift was in return for a night spent with each of them.

Odin knew now that this woman's true name was not Gullweig. It was not a true giantess who had gone to the dwarfs for Brisingamen, but the Vanir goddess of love, Freya, in the form of a giant-goddess. The giants were not so spoiled in their tastes as to love precious objects with such passion.

The Aesir grew impatient with Gullweig. Even cheery Thor stopped talking to her and stomped off in a roll of thunder to kill a giant or two. Even cunning Loki's smile faded. Gullweig's talk was all about her gold necklace, her jewels, the shine of her hair, the elaborate gold thread of her garments. Not a word did she let fall about ordinary things – otters, cattle, boats, salmon, snow.

Was she trying to anger the Aesir? Did the Vanir want war? Odin was not sure, but he and the rest of the Aesir felt a mounting disgust for Gullweig. Her presence and her talk threatened to alter Asgard, as they had altered Midgard. The Aesir finally surrounded her, and at a signal they all threw their glittering spears at her.

At her, through her, and out at the other side, as harmlessly as if they had drifted through sunlight! Gullweig laughed till her slender sides shook. For Gullweig *was* Freya, the Vanir witch-goddess, the goddess of war and love, and the lover of gold.

The Aesir built a huge fire in Odin's hall, Valhall, and threw Freya-Gullweig into it. But it was like throwing light into fire. When the flames died down, Freya-Gullweig stepped out unharmed, flushed and beautiful as if she had stepped out of a hot bath.

"So that is how you treat a messenger of the Vanir!" she cried. "Now there will be war between the Aesir and the Vanir!"

And with that threatening cry she vanished.

And while the Aesir were still debating whether or not she had come from Jotunheim, the flashing shields of the Vanir came hurtling down out of the sky

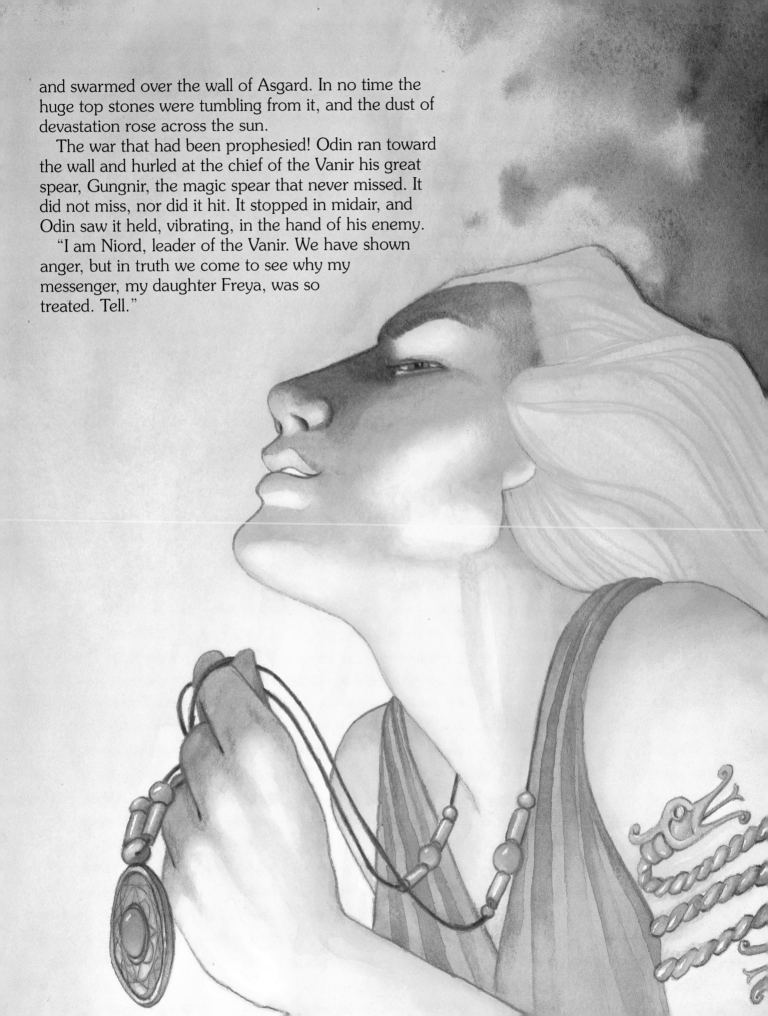

and swarmed over the wall of Asgard. In no time the huge top stones were tumbling from it, and the dust of devastation rose across the sun.

The war that had been prophesied! Odin ran toward the wall and hurled at the chief of the Vanir his great spear, Gungnir, the magic spear that never missed. It did not miss, nor did it hit. It stopped in midair, and Odin saw it held, vibrating, in the hand of his enemy.

"I am Niord, leader of the Vanir. We have shown anger, but in truth we come to see why my messenger, my daughter Freya, was so treated. Tell."

When Odin told Niord about Freya-Gullweig's trickery and the fatal effect of her gold-talk on men and women, Niord was silent. He realized that Freya-Gullweig had tricked the Vanir as well. Away from Vanaheim, her homeland, her lust for beautiful jewels and dazzling gold had become uncontrollable.

Niord raised his arm as a signal and his voice resounded like ten peals of thunder in the darkened sky over Asgard: "Let there be no war between the Aesir and the Vanir. The enemies of the gods are not each other, but glimmering ice giants, dark cliff ogres, trouble-trolls, that whole race and their timeless treacheries."

Before the echoes of his rumbling voice had finally died away along the walls, the fighting had stopped. It was over almost before it had begun. Odin and Niord strode forward and embraced.

Odin spoke. "Our one enemy is evil. Our only foes are the giant-race."

Niord spoke. "We must join our powers in one power. We must find a road through our anger. We must carry peace along it."

Odin felt the glancing light of wisdom pierce him. "Let Aesir become Vanir, Vanir become Aesir."

And so true peace came. It was agreed that long-legged Honir should go with the Vanir and be one of them; and Niord himself, first of the Vanir, would be one of the Aesir. Freya, the Vanir enchantress, brought her beauty to the Aesir. And Mimir, the wisest of the Aesir, took his wisdom to the Vanir.

The gods were united, one race. For the moment, Odin's mind was at rest.

20

Giant-slaughtering

*T*hor and Loki were sitting under Yggdrasil. Thor was finishing his breakfast of oats and herring.

Thor wiped his hand across his mouth. "I'm going," he said to Loki.

"Where to?"

"Jotunheim. Giant-splintering."

"To Jotunheim? Now?"

"My hammer Mjollnir is restless. Idleness irritates him. He wants to be wielded. He hungers to harm giants, to be hurled at some furlong-length frost-face. He longs to crack some cliff-heads."

Loki was curious. It would be entertaining to visit giant-land in the company of large-hearted, not-so-large-brained Thor.

"Giant-crunching takes cunning, Thor," Loki said, "not just thunder-strength. And there are still many of them, roaming the white wastes and clambering the cliffs. I will come to help you. You bring the brawn, I can carry the brains…"

"And the food and drink." Thor threw Loki the heavy food bag and grinned good-humoredly. Loki's teasing was just a flea-itch. Loki was unreliable, but his cunning might be worth having on a trip.

Thor's servant Thialfi tethered his goats to the cart, then Thor took up the rein of twisted silver, and the three of them were off – Thor the giant-slayer, Loki the cunning, and Thialfi the serving youth. With a storm of hail moving in front of them like a white shield, they rumbled out of Asgarth. Behind the lashing hail the sky was the bronze of Thor's beard, and below, along the rough plain, the old cart went bumping and juddering, its clatter and thump shaking the space under the clouds. Lightning glittered from the axle, lighting up the sides of snow-covered mountains, throwing its brilliance across the flint-gray fjords, over into the green woods of Midgard.

They came to Ifing, the river that separates Asgard from Jotunheim. Leaving Thor's cart behind, they ferried over and started walking.

Thor had often visited Jotunheim, to kill giants or do grievous bodily harm to them. When, far away in Midgard and Asgard, humans and gods heard distant tearing and cracking noises, like avalanches rumbling or glaciers splintering into the sea, they knew what it meant. Thor was at work. Wearing the belt that doubled his strength and his iron gauntlets, he was sending his hammer, Mjollnir, whizzing at the heads of giants.

Thor made the world safe. This visit was meant to be another routine giant-battering trip.

In Jotunheim, Loki, Thor, and Thialfi tramped over a plain to a forest. They walked in the forest for the rest of the day without seeing a single dwelling. The sun began to glow red through the trees. They would have to spend the night in the forest. They started to look for a place to sleep under the immense beeches and oaks.

After a while Thor heard a distant shout, "Over here!"

Helped by the glow of the stars, Thor made his way to where Loki was standing, pointing. Loki had found a clearing.

"Brains, you see!" Loki said.

They made out the outline of a building. It was not much taller than they were, but curved up at the top, like a loaf, with a dark entrance that took up the whole front of the building. It was open, so in they went, throwing themselves down in exhaustion and dropping off to sleep right away.

In the middle of the night, they were shaken awake. The floor of the hall had tilted over like the deck of a

ship in a storm, and they were sliding to one side, over what felt like polished leather. Thump. Then the floor tilted the other way. Slide, swivel, thump, in a tangle of arms and legs they piled against the side wall. Then quiet again.

Thialfi suggested they go farther into the house, so they followed the bend of the walls around into a curved side-room that was narrower than the entrance. If there was any more rocking and rolling, they would only shift a few feet. They slept through till dawn, when Thor was first to wake, disturbed by the din of birds.

He went outside into the bright sun. He was in the middle of a yawn and stretch when he heard a slow heaving sound behind him, like a wave breaking across a beach. Thor turned around and found himself staring into the biggest giant-jaw he had ever stared into. It was open like a cavern. The wave sound he had heard was the giant breathing.

This giant was twice as big as any giant Thor or Loki or Thialfi had ever seen. A few hundred yards of sleeping body stretched into the trees and disappeared in the dawn-mists, where the feet must have been hiding. The snoring opened the giant's mouth and closed it, pushing a drawbridge of black beard down and up again. A tall fence of teeth shone in the sun.

The giant grunted and woke.

"Ah," he said, getting to his feet, rising up into the treetops, so the mist swirled around his head. He looked down. "Thor himself. And Loki. And Thialfi. Good morning. I am Skrymir. A giant, as you notice. Did you enjoy your snooze in my glove? Now, shall I help you carry your sack of food? Have no fear. Through magic we saw you coming. We decided not to fight you this time, but to challenge you to friendly duels. I offer you safe passage to Jotunheim. I will even accompany you part of the way."

"Glove? Glove?" Thor was scratching his head. He couldn't figure it out, but Loki was pointing back to the place where the "hall" had been.

Thor had come with his iron gauntlets to do some hammer hurling, not to give a giant his food bag to carry, but while he was thinking of a way out Loki accepted. Loki, protected by Thor's tremendous strength, was not thinking of danger, only of mischief and entertainment.

With Skrymir leading the way, they walked the whole day. Thor, Loki, and Thialfi often had to run a few steps to keep up with Skrymir's huge, slow-motion stride. They were still in the forest when they stopped for the night. Skrymir slipped the bag of food from his shoulder, stretched out, and went right to sleep.

The three from Asgard were hungry, but when Thialfi, then Loki, then Thor tried to untie the knot at the neck of the bag, they couldn't – Skrymir had tightened it up so that it was like a knot of iron.

They had to wake Skrymir if they wanted supper. "Skrymir! Wake up!" First they just said his name loudly and nudged him. That was no good. They shouted and shook his arm. Skrymir slept on. Thor gave Skrymir a gentle tap on the shin with his hammer. No use. He clambered along up to his knee and dropped a sharp, light blow on his kneecap, which gave out a thin clank. Skrymir scratched his knee and slept on.

Thor was getting cross. He buckled on his strength-doubling belt and pulled on his iron gauntlets. Then he wound himself up as if he were going to throw the hammer a hundred miles back to Asgard and let loose a fierce, whistling swing on the top of Skrymir's head. BOIOING – Skrymir's skull clanged like a bell. This time he nearly woke up.

He yawned. "Yaaarrrmmm…was that?" he muttered, half asleep, scratching his head. "Yeeaarm… leaf…head." Then he turned over and went to sleep again.

Thor, Loki, and Thialfi had to go without supper and couldn't sleep comfortably. Around midnight they were roused by a roaring wind. Thor opened his eyes to see the giant's open mouth gaping a few yards away. The gale and storm-noise came from Skrymir's open mouth.

"Stop snoring!" Thor roared, and once again, even more fiercely than before, he swung Mjollnir, this time at a place just above Skrymir's left eye.

BOIOIOING – like a shield dropped on the floor.

Skrymir stirred and yawned out a surge of stinking warm breath that rolled Thor and Loki over like bits of

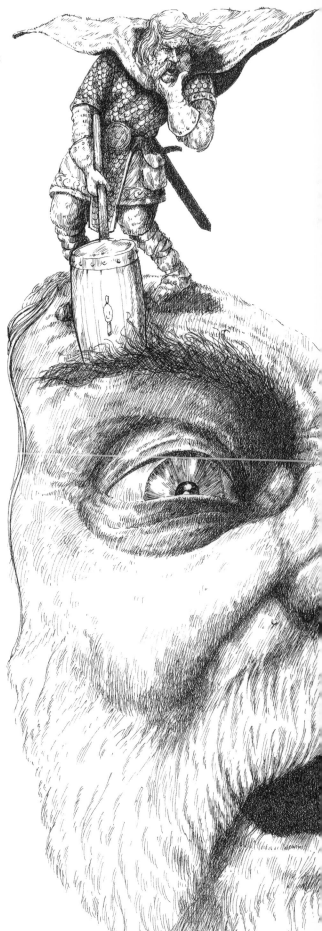

25

straw. As he went back to sleep, Skrymir mumbled, "Big...acorn..."

The night passed slowly. At sunrise, Thor, madder than ever at not having had anything to eat or any sleep, decided to send Skrymir to the next world.

Winding Mjollnir so far around him that the head of the hammer appeared in front of him again, Thor unleashed the most terrifying, explosive swing Loki had ever seen him throw, and Mjollnir was a faint blur of light.

BOIOIOIOING – like a deep gong.

"Pagh," Skrymir said, waking and getting to his feet. He wiped his hand over the top of his head and looked at it, then he looked up into the trees. "These filthy birds.

"Now, isn't it time you were off? You haven't far to go to Jotunheim. But before you set out let me tell you a thing or two. I know you think I'm a big fellow, but you'll meet bigger giants in the hall of giants, Utgard, so be careful. Don't try to be too clever when you get there, and whatever you do, don't boast. If you had any sense you'd turn around and go back, but if you're determined to see Utgard, that's the way, over yonder, where the sun is shining on the snow. I'm off to the north. Farewell."

And off went Skrymir, with their provision bag thrown over his shoulders.

"My eyes must be lying, like false mirrors," Thor said. "Never before has Mjollnir failed to end a giant's life."

"The giants must have practiced some magic," Loki said, "or else your huge strength is failing you, Thor. You can't hurl your hammer till the end of time anyway."

Thor arrives at Utgard

Thor and Loki and the young man Thialfi walked all morning, alongside lakes and across mountains. Early in the afternoon, they saw on the snowy plain a grim-looking castle of glimmering green-gray ice. It seemed to be only a mile or two away, but it took them all afternoon to walk there. At nightfall they arrived at the gates and stood staring up at huge, shining walls that rode up away from them into the sky, so that the icy towers disappeared in clouds.

The gate was thick with rime, and as they all pushed at it their hands stuck to its cold. They could not push it open, but in the gate there was a small door with iron bars, wide enough apart for them to squeeze between. Once inside they heard a din of voices, and following the noise they came into a huge hall, where giants sat at benches, eating and drinking. No one noticed them at first, then the King of Utgard, Utgard-Loki, saw them. He pointed down at them.

"Well, look what we have here – urchins from Asgard, minigods from Midgard. Here we have Thor and Loki – Loki of the same name as I but not of the same family. And Thialfi, Thor's young servant. Thor and Loki, we have given you safe passage, because sometimes we admit visitors. But it is only if they have a great talent to please us with. What will you do to earn the right not to be driven away?"

There was loud laughter and banging of metal mugs on tables. The din hammered into Thor's and Loki's eardrums.

Loki spoke first. "I have a mountainous appetite. I can eat faster than ten wolves. No one in Utgard hall can eat faster, that I'll wager."

Utgard-Loki said, "Well, we have our own champion champer, the great-girthed gormandizer, Logi the Large. Logi, will you do a dire duel of juicy jaws with the Aesir's all-consuming Loki the Little? Will you enter the eating arena with the fodder-annihilator from Asgard?"

There was more roaring and mug-banging, as Logi stepped forward.

Utgard-Loki ordered servants to bring into the hall a long wooden trench filled with meat. Then Loki was stood at one end and Logi at the other.

Utgard-Loki banged the end of his spear on the floor.

"They're off!"

The combatants went at the trench as if their mouths hadn't met a minnow in a month. In only a few minutes their slavering, juicy chins met in the middle. Loki looked around. Was he Logi's equal in eating?

No! While Loki had been eating the meat but leaving the bones, down into the depths of Logi vanished half the meat, half the bones, and half the wooden trench! Loki felt cheated. How was he to compete against a giant who chewed timber and browsed on bones?

Next, Utgard-Loki asked Thialfi what his talent was.

"I can run like the wind."

Utgard-Loki called over a young lad named Hugi.

"Once around the hall. Ready?" Hugi and Thialfi nodded. "Go!"

The giants roared them on as they skidded around the ends of benches, sending stacked spears and piled chain mail flying. Hugi was far ahead at the finish, but Utgard-Loki said that Thialfi was faster than anyone else who had visited Utgard.

"Practice against the fastest winds, and you might be able to give Hugi a good race in the future."

It was Thor's turn.

"What duel for you, Thor?" asked Utgard-Loki.

"A drinking bout for me! A wrestle with the thirstiest giant-throat!" And Thor gave a great thunder-roar of a laugh.

Two cupbearers carried in a curved drinking horn that was as long as two pine trees. They offered it to Thor. It was brimming full.

"It is good drinking to drain this off in one pull," said Utgard-Loki. "Some drinkers down it in two, but only puny throats stop more than once."

Thor lifted the horn, and a tide of sparkling golden beer flowed into his throat. The first long gulps were easy, then his breath started to run out. The giants nudged each other and grinned, puffing out their cheeks in imitation. But on and on Thor drank, forcing himself, his lungs burning for lack of breath. He could feel a furnace rising in his face as his breath failed. "Haaaaa!" He finally gulped at the air, like a drowning man at the surface. As the horn banged back on the table, Thor saw how much was left.

It was nearly full! Almost spilling over!

"You can drink quite well," Utgard-Loki said, "though not as deeply as we expected. But surely you will empty it at the second draught?"

Thor took a huge grab of breath and began again. Glug, glug, glug, glug, glug, glug...on and on and on, for much longer than before. When the horn slammed down it still felt heavy, though Thor was sure it must be nearly empty. He peered in. The beer was a finger's width below the rim!

"One more?" asked Utgard-Loki.

And even after one more long drink, Thor had hardly made any impression on the level in the drinking horn. He was puzzled. The fellows at the tables were grinning and banging their mugs on the tabletops.

Utgard-Loki spoke. "Thor, you are not the immense ale-guzzler we expected. Here among the giants you wouldn't be celebrated as a serious swallower. Is there anything else you can do, to redeem yourself in our eyes?"

Thor didn't reply. He was puzzled. He was staring at the drinking horn, trying to understand. Loki had an unpleasant smirk on his face. He was delighted that Thor had been beaten.

"Can you wrestle?" Utgard-Loki asked.

"Can a rooster crow? Can hail batter? Try me with one of these big fellows here. I may be smaller, but you'll hear your answer when he thumps to the floor."

"Thor, these great-chested fellows would be angry if I asked them to wrestle with a smaller being, however strong. But here's my old foster mother, Elli. She likes a good wrestle, and she's floored opponents stronger-looking than you."

A wizened creature, grinning and toothless, shuffled forward into the torchlight. She went straight up to Thor and took him by the arm. Thor stepped back in alarm. "Wrestle with...! What do you think...?" He got no further with his spluttering protest. The old woman pushed her foot behind his ankle and spun him to the ground, as if he were no heavier than a feather. A roar of laughter went along the hall, the loudest that day. The mugs were clattered even louder on the tables.

Thor leaped up, mad at being put down, mad at the laughter, even madder that he had to wrestle an old woman. He caught her by the wrists and tightened his grip, ready to throw her, then abruptly his arms were jerked down, his head plunged somewhere between his knees, and he went dizzily upside down and felt himself slide with a crash into what sounded like a pile of shields. He staggered up and threw his arms around her waist. They swayed to and fro, and Thor nearly pushed her back down, but then his hammer-wielding arm was thrown behind him, so far around that he thought it was coming off at the shoulder. Then he was down on one knee, unable to move. He twisted around and looked up into the crone's face, and couldn't believe its wrinkles and toothless grin.

"Enough," Utgard-Loki said. "And enough of that entertainment. Thor, Loki, Thialfi, you have pleased us with your brave efforts. You have tried, and you have showed that you might win against weaker opponents. Now it is time to relax and eat and drink. In the morning I will show you the way back toward Asgarth."

For once, Thor scowled. He couldn't enjoy his eating and drinking. His drinking strength was leaving him; an old giant-woman had wrestled him to the floor. Loki was angry too, especially with Thor, for asking him to come to Utgard and be humiliated. He was beginning to think that, if the giants were really stronger than the Aesir, perhaps he would join them. Loki wanted to be on the right side if there was a battle.

At the first sign of dawn, Thor, Loki, and Thialfi got up, had breakfast, and began to make themselves ready. Utgard-Loki came to see them off. "Well, has your journey here been worth all the trouble? Has Utgard impressed you? Have you ever met a more powerful king than me?"

"We don't like being beaten and being made fools of. Otherwise we had a fine visit."

"Don't be resentful, Thor. I will tell you the truth now. I have deceived all three of you. Loki, Thialfi, you have great power in eating and running. Thor, you are a great drinker, and stronger than you know. I have deceived you with spells. It was I who met you as Skrymir in the wood. I fastened up your bag with iron wire. When you hit me with Mjollnir, I sent the shuddering power of the blows skidding off into the surrounding hills. On your way back you will see three lakes glittering at the bottom of steep-sided craters. They are the craters that Thor's Mjollnir made in the hills of Jotunheim, when he tried to scatter my sleeping skull to the stars.

"Loki, you were competing against Fire, disguised as Logi. Nothing can consume and devour like Fire. Thialfi, you thought you were beaten by Hugi, but you were racing against Thought. There is nothing quicker than Thought, which can run around the world in less time than you leap a stream.

"And now you, Thor. First let me warn you, do not come here again. We should fear your coming. We laughed, but in truth your drinking made us fearful. When you supped ale from the horn, the other end was sucking up the sea. You were drinking the sea itself, Thor, and we saw with great fear that after a while its level began to drop. You will see, when you come to the shore, that the beach at low tide is wider, because the sea now holds less water.

"And when you wrestled, it was amazing that you held out for so long, because you were wrestling with Old Age herself, who brings everyone to their knees. If I had not used all this magic to defend my stronghold, who knows, you might have conquered Utgard."

Instead of being flattered by Utgard-Loki's praise, Thor was furious at being deluded by magic trickery. He raised his hammer to the clouds, but Utgard-Loki faded away, and Mjollnir only swung down into the earth with an enormous thump like thunder. The ground shook for a whole minute. A new valley had been plowed into Jotunheim.

There was no sign of Utgard-Loki, or of his ice-gray stronghold, Utgard. Thor and Loki saw only the wide open plain, with the forest at its western edge. Beyond the forest was the coast, and the firth of Ifing that they had crossed a few days before. They set off toward the warm fires of Asgard.

Balder's Death

Balder was the god of light. The sun on the fells, a scarf of flowers at the fjord's edge, gleaming eagle eggs, everything that shone with natural beauty reminded gods and men of Balder.

He was Odin's son, and the sun in his father's sky. He was the most-loved god. He knew he was wise, but no fleck of pride marked him. He had the same speech for prince and plowman, a kind speech, soft as thaw-water running over stones.

But the most-loved god began to have dreams of hatred and evil. In the dreams, darkness came swirling across the sun. Pale creatures poured their stinking breath into his face and raised jeweled daggers over him. They turned into snarling wolves and he found himself running from them over Bifrost, the rainbow bridge linking Asgard to earth. Under his slow feet the dreaming Balder felt the bridge sag and begin to fail, and it sang like struck metal. He fell to the sea, but somehow set out in his boat. Then cliff giants, iceberg high, heaved hills into the harbors and firths, and the boat overturned, and Balder dreamed of drowning.

Balder told his dreams to Nanna, his wife, then to Odin, and to Frigga, his mother. They were afraid for Balder. Odin first sent his ravens out to discover who intended harm to Balder, then he himself, on his eight-legged horse Sleipnir, set out for Niflheim, the icy world of death. He might learn some truth from the dead.

He went through Niflheim and came near to the high halls of Hel. The fierce watch-hound, Garm, howled in his way. Odin sang a rune-charm against it, and sang the beast down till it cowered. Odin passed and entered the hall. He saw the benches and coats of mail waiting for warriors. He saw cauldrons of beer brewed ready, waiting for the newly dead to feast on them, shields covering them. Who was to die?

He knew the grave of a prophetess nearby. He went to the mound and chanted a second rune-charm, singing her out of the ground to speak to him.

A twisted face rose before him.

"Who drags me from under the earth? I was buried in snow and hammered by rain. Who?"

Odin spoke. "For whom is the beer brewed? Who is to die?"

"I am loath to speak. Let me cease before I begin."

"For whom is the beer brewed? Tell."

"For many the beer is brewed. And for Balder the beer is brewed, for Balder the blameless. I was loath to speak. Let me cease."

She was gone. Odin drew his cloak around him, as if against the cold of knowing that his son was to die. But he did not know when, or how, and could not compel the prophetess to reveal more.

He returned to Asgard and told Frigga the little he knew. The ravens returned with no knowledge of harm to Balder. Odin summoned the gods.

"My ravens have beaten their wings over all the world to find who threatens Balder. Nowhere have they found, on any misty crag, in any blue crevasse, between any sundering floes, on any weed-hung stones on the seabed, one lurking being – god or dwarf, giant or black elf – whose thought holds a dagger to Balder's heart. I begin to trust the future time again."

But trust was not certainty. Odin and the rest of the Aesir were still fearful for his son and needed to make sure that he would come to no harm.

Frigga, Balder's mother, spoke. "Let everything take a vow to protect Balder. Odin, let me, Balder's loving mother, journey around the worlds and collect vows from every being, and let me scratch them all in wood or stone to be a record and memory."

35

It was agreed. Frigga went first to fire. She heard it talking where men were cooking fish, among some sticks at the edge of a firth. Frigga knelt and spoke to fire, and fire promised that if its flames came near Balder they would turn away, just as they did before water. Next Frigga spoke to water. Water said that none of its shapes would harm Balder, just as its waves never swallowed great cliffs, or grasped gannets to their death, just as its dank dew never drowned thistles.

Iron spoke ringingly to Frigga. Its axes would glance sideways around Balder, its spears would spin short. From all the first forces of the world, Frigga slowly gathered her harvest of promises. Stone would shatter, ice melt, lightning delay, fierce winds relent, rather than harm Balder.

Then Frigga went to the creatures of earth and asked them to make the same vow. The adder agreed to writhe away out of Balder's path, the white bear to sheathe its claws and swim the other way. While Balder was near, no flooded river would rise by a leaf's thickness, no unsteady ice topple toward him, no disease reach out to touch him.

After her long journey, Frigga finally returned. "Balder is safe," she said, and she told Odin the list of the vows. Odin was now sure Balder was safe. Nanna was sure. The rest of the Aesir were sure. Odin put his certainty to the test. He pressed the point of a small dagger against Balder's smooth cheek. The dagger glided aside like a bubble around a rock in a stream.

Then Odin lit a torch and threw it toward Balder. It went out with a hiss and fell to the floor. The watching gods stared. Then they laughed. Here was a new game.

One by one they tested the vows of fire, rock, metal. One by one the stones, the arrows, and the spears shattered in midair or clanged down or were thrown aside like straw in a wind. Hurled fire met a ring of cold, hurled ice hissed out like a falling star. The gods roared. Nothing as funny had been seen in Asgard.

They made their games more amusing. A wolf was set at Balder. It jumped, fell back yelping, and cringed its way out into the snow. The gods howled with it. A bear was unleashed. He rumbled toward Balder, sniffed down at him, waved a paw vaguely near Balder's head, then jerked his own head to one side, swayed, and turned to look dimly toward the gods. Then he lumbered off on all fours.

The gods roared and roared. There would have been cruelty in their excitement if Balder had felt any pain, but he was protected by the vows of all the world.

One of the gods was watching without much amusement. It was Loki. The trickster-god disliked the sudden popularity of Balder. Balder had been loved and admired before, but this was different. He was making the gods roar with laughter. He was at the center of their games.

Loki looked across at Frigga, who was smiling. An unpleasant thought crawled quickly into Loki's dark mind, and he went across to Frigga.

"Frigga, is this a wise game? Is Balder safe from all the threats of the world? Will no rock ever topple near him, will every surge of the sea restrain itself when Balder sails?"

Frigga looked deeply at Loki, and saw his eyes glittering like an adder's. Loki's passion was to make trouble, but surely no trouble could come from this. Yet she feared his cunning and jealousy.

She thought back to her long journey across the world, into Niflheim and Jotunheim and … yes, everything had promised – air, sand, rock, plants, birds, insects, fish, water, fire, ice, snakes, snow, everything.

"Everything in the world has sworn to protect Balder," she boasted. "I have asked everything. I have been to every…"

No, not everything. Her voice trailed off as she remembered. One evening, exhausted from spending the day scouring for promises in the mountains, she had seen, high above her, the one thing she had not gathered a vow from; a mistletoe, a bush rooted in an oak, not on earth, a bush without spines and far away from their home. Exhausted and trusting the mistletoe's harmlessness, Frigga had thrown herself down on the grass and had fallen into a deep, peaceful sleep.

So, there still existed in the world one thing that had not promised to protect Balder.

Loki saw Frigga hesitate. "What's wrong, Frigga? You suddenly seem uncertain?"

Loki had guessed her thought. But no danger could come from the harmless mistletoe, or from Loki knowing it had not promised. And Frigga was proud... "Of all the million things in the world, the only one that has not promised is a small bush without spines that grows far, far from here."

"What bush is that?"

"The mistletoe."

Loki's eyes glittered again. "Well then, you must be pleased with your work. Balder must surely be safe, if that is the only thing that has not vowed protection to him." Loki smiled, but it was a cold, thinking smile, like a fading sun.

Loki slid from the hall unnoticed, out into the night. He soon found the mountain and the mistletoe. He cut a branch from it, shaped a small spear, and set off back to Asgard.

Now Balder had a brother, Hoder, who was blind. There was as much sad darkness in his world as there was loving light in Balder's. He couldn't join in the games, but he enjoyed being in the hall with the gods, listening in his darkness to their shouts and laughter. As Hoder sat by the fire, he would feel a trencher of meat, a mug of beer, guided into his hand.

Loki had just come back into the hall, carrying a short spear. He had only been gone a few minutes. He looked across to blind Hoder, sitting by the fire. He saw how Hoder smiled at the din, his useless eyes wandering blankly.

If Hoder had been able to look across at Loki he would have noticed the fierce glow in his eyes. It was the malice of Loki, naked as molten lava.

The fire roared higher, drumming like a volcano, as if in warning.

But none of the gods was alert. It was late, and they had drunk too many jugs of beer. It was time to play the last game of testing Balder.

The gods hurled their joke projectiles. As usual, missiles and weapons broke up in midair. A torch fizzed out, plates cracked apart, jugs tinkled to the floor, stones skidded off sideways. Every failed throw made the gods roar. Thor even threw his hammer, Mjollnir, knowing it would whiz around Balder like a bee around a flower. It did, and Thor collapsed with laughter in a corner. Balder tolerated it all, cruel though he felt it was. The gods didn't think it was cruel, because nothing harmed Balder. Nothing could harm Balder.

A hand touched Hoder's hand. "Join in the game. Throw this tiny spear." Hoder recognized Loki's voice.

"Hoder will play," Loki shouted. There was surprise and laughter in every face as Hoder lifted his little spear. From his place by the fire he hurled it. It sped through the air, the newly peeled wood gleaming like Balder's skin.

Balder cried out, and staggered. The gods laughed louder. Balder was acting the fool for the blind Hoder, adding to their fun.

Balder fell. The gods roared louder. Balder didn't move. The gods laughed and laughed, uncontrollably, but when Balder didn't move, and still didn't move, they fell silent.

Slowly the fuddled gods took it in. The spear that Hoder had thrown had hit Balder and hurt him. Thor's huge hammer had been harmless, but Hoder's small spear had buried itself deep in Balder's side, and Balder lay dying. The light of the world was dying.

The gods turned to Hoder, who stood grinning, thinking that the silence was part of the game. Odin, seeing into the truth, looked around for Loki, but the treacherous god had already faded deep into the night.

And so Balder died, and Loki fled from Asgard.

The body of Balder was placed in a boat with his sword and rich jewels around him. The Aesir assembled on the strand, and the air was full of grief. In the afternoon, other beings came to join the great lament. There were gentle elves and blear-eyed dwarfs, who for once ventured out of the dark caves where they hammered out jewelry and precious rings. There were even frost giants and cliff giants, weeping immense tears.

In the midst of it all, Nanna, Balder's wife, swayed and fell to the sand. Broken by grief, she died. The gods placed her body in the boat beside Balder.

When it was evening, a flaming torch – like the torches that had fallen harmlessly in the game – was thrown into the bow of the boat. As fire began to crackle and take hold, the Aesir hauled the ship to the edge of the water and with a huge shove tried to launch it toward the setting sun. But there was such a weight of silver and gold on board that they couldn't move it. Or perhaps the boat, knowing it carried Balder on his last journey, was reluctant to start from

the shore. Only with the help of giants was it rolled down the beach and heaved forward over the water.

At first the prow broke the waves as if men were rowing, then the ship began to drift. The sail filled out in the wind, then flames climbed around and burned holes in it like paper. Then the mast burst into flames, and in seconds the ship was a bed of fire. It steamed and disappeared. Balder, best of the gods, and Nanna had gone from the world.

From afar, in Jotunheim, the treacherous Loki watched it all, knowing he could never return to Asgard.

The Aesir were numb. Odin remembered the priestess in Hel. What other deaths were being prepared?

The Aesir were grief-stricken. If only Balder could be brought back, if only brilliant light could be brought back to the sky, glistening freshness to the shining flowers, dazzle to the rock pools, intense color to the feathers of birds. If only they could stop the glaze of dullness spreading over everything.

Frigga spoke. "Perhaps, when we tell the ruler of Niflheim what has happened, Hel will return him from the dead. If one of the Aesir will take the dark path down to Hel, he can speak all the good we know of Balder. Then Balder and Nanna might be restored to us. Whoever takes the path to Hel and brings Balder back will have my love."

Hermod, a son of Odin and Frigga, spoke. "I will take the dark road to Hel."

Odin lent him his horse, Sleipnir, and Hermod departed. He went down under earth, by the same terrible road Odin had ridden, through freezing mists, along gray valleys. He came to Hel hall and watched troops of men newly dead assembling there, their faces empty of life. He saw Hel herself lying on her couch, half-hidden by the curtains of Glimmering Misfortune.

Hel rose and came forward, slowly. She spoke. Her speech was as slow as her step.

"You are too soon. You live. It is not your time."

"I come only to speak to you. Balder, beloved of all things, is here, taken from us by trickery. Odin asks, do you wish to hold Balder, when all things weep for him?

Odin wishes that you may return him to us."

Hel spoke. "Do all things weep for Balder? Was there none who wished his death? Let the Aesir send messengers to tell all the things of the worlds of Balder's end, and watch if they weep. If every force in the worlds and every being and creature weeps for him, let Balder return. They can weep him out of Hel. Till then, let him stay."

The Aesir sent messengers to every place in the worlds. Odin sent his ravens, Hugin and Mugin. Frigga wandered the earth as well.

Soon they began to return. The messengers said that everything they met wept. The worlds wept – metal, stone, water, rivers, deserts, mountains, seas and fire, the great winds, hurrying animals, and birds crowding the cliffs. Everything wept for Balder.

But just as Frigga had overlooked the one thing that could harm Balder, now the messengers, the ravens and Frigga had overlooked the one being that had not wept.

Then some of the messengers remembered. On their way back through Jotunheim to Asgard, they had found a giantess asleep in a cave. All the other giants had wept for Balder, and when the messengers asked this one if she did, they expected only one answer.

But no. "Weep for Balder? Why should I weep for Balder? He never wept for me. Go back to Asgard and tell Odin and the rest that Thokk, the giantess, refuses to join in their games!"

Nothing could be done to change her mind. When the messengers reached Asgard and told Odin, he went to his high throne and gazed across the worlds. He knew whom he expected to see.

Far away in Jotunheim, sitting outside a cave, he saw the giantess. She had called herself Thokk, but the being Odin saw gazing back toward Asgard had the cold smile and flame-filled eyes of Loki.

Ragnarok – the end of the gods

Balder the beautiful had died. He could not be brought back from the country of the dead. Loki had disappeared to join the giants. Evil had entered Asgard.

Odin went to the prophetess Volva again. He gave her golden arm-rings and gems. He wanted to know the future.

"What do you see, Volva, prophetess? What do you see in the future?"

Volva spoke. "I see it all. I say it all. Do not break the chain of my saying."

"I will stay silent."

"I see the fate of things. I fathom the future, and further. I see far and wide around the worlds.

"The end is beginning. Ragnarok is coming. I see no summer, only a great winter, a white wind age. I see fierce winds roam like wolves. Three winters follow in one great winter.

"That is the first age. I see then an ax age, a sword age. Shields shatter. Brother fights brother, fathers battle with sons.

"I see the Valkyry Women, Choosers of the Dead. They gather in the air in glinting flocks. They are riding the sky to Midgard to choose who will die.

"A wolf age. War. Women, men murdered. Brothers fight brothers; they betray their sisters' sons. The spears of men spare no one. The dragon Nidhogg gnaws naked corpses. Women and men, lost, wade waist-deep through swift water that swirls with sword-like cold. Murderous men escape, and those who betray children, those who betray friends' wives.

"I see a terrible brood of wolves – Fenrir, Garm, Skoll. Fenrir rends men. I see the wolf feed on the flesh of men fallen in battle. The benches of the gods are smeared with blood. I see it. I fathom the future and further. The wolf Garm bays at the moon. The wolf Skoll slavers after the weakening sun. The sun of summer grows dark…"

Odin could not be silent. "What next? What next?"

"The hall of the gods shakes. The evil giants gather. Garm breaks free of his fetters. All bonds are broken. Rivers break loose; winds howl indoors. Under the sea the Midgard Serpent writhes his thousand-leagues-long body, thrashes his tail. Mountainous waves batter the shores of the worlds. Sea-eagles scream.

"I see far into what is fated to be. I see the end of the gods.

"Heimdall, watchman of the gods, blares his horn, sounding the downfall of the gods, summoning them to battle. The blaring of gleaming old Gjallarhorn sounds their doom. Heimdall blows loud, and horror spreads in the halls of the Aesir. The towering Tree of All the Worlds, Yggdrasil, trembles, its leaves sighing loudly.

"Terrible trouble has come to the Aesir. In the east the giants are raging in uproar. Deep in the fastness of the fells the wise dwarfs groan with grief. The leader of the giants strides from the east, in war gear. A ship sails from the east. Loki is steering it. Mindless hordes of giants wade in its wake.

"Swart, the ruler of fire, comes from the south, his sword flaming red like the sun. Yggdrasil bursts into

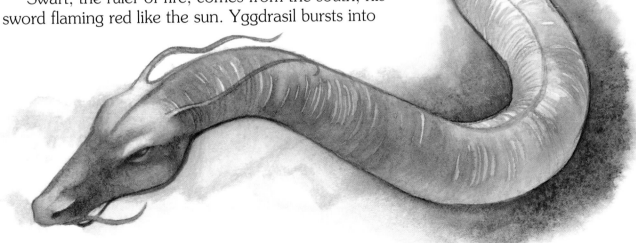

45

flames. The tall hills totter; gods and giants stagger.
Men go wandering from their homes and end in Hel.
The sky splits open.

"Battle begins between the Aesir and the giants.
Heimdall strikes Loki dead to the heart, in revenge for
Balder. Then Odin dies, fighting against the wolf Fenrir.
Odin speaks his last words, then Fenrir takes him.

"Thor wades into the fray, wielding Mjollnir. The
grisly serpent that girdles the earth gapes at him. Thor,
the guardian of Midgard, the great dragon-ender and
troll-mauler, slays the Midgard Serpent, then falls back
nine steps and lies there, splattered with poison. Giants
and gods go to their deaths together.

"The earth sinks under the sea, the sun goes dark.
The bright stars fall out of the sky. Scalding steam
gushes out of the ground, and raging fire. Drumming
flames wind thunderously up to the darkness.

"But I see further. Further on, and a better future. I
see green fields with things growing and grass waving.
I see land rising out of the sea. Streams shine in the
sun, rivers tumble from the fells, the eagle flies over
them, calling.

"I see a few of the Aesir meet on Shining Plain. The
sons of Vili and Ve are there, and the sons of Thor.
They find Mjollnir lying in the grass. They talk about
the might of the Midgard Serpent. They talk of the
doom that came to the world.

"All the world comes again. I see it. In Midgard
two of the human race live again, Lif and Lifthrasir.
They survived hidden in Yggdrasil, fed from its dews. I
see their children playing in the shade of Yggdrasil.

"In the grass the new gods find gold figures, the gold
pieces of old. They marvel at them, and play games
again in the garth. Cattle wander, corn grows on
unsown acres.

"Good drives back evil, and Balder comes again. He
and blind Hoder and the sons of Odin's brothers live
once more in the wide home of the winds, in a hall
fairer than the sun, thatched with red gold. The new
gods live there, without grief or guilt, in happiness."

The priestess fell silent. Odin watched her fade into
the earth. At last he knew what was to be.

Notes

Aesir (say Eye'-zeer) (p. 7, 12, 17-18, 35-36, 41-43, 45-46)
The gods who live in Asgard. Odin is their leader.

Asgard (say Az'-gard) (p. 10, 12, 15-16, 18-20, 23, 25, 27, 32-36, 40-44)
The world of the Aesir gods.

Balder (say Borl'-da) (p. 34-44, 46)
The most beautiful of the gods, and the son of Odin and Frigga.

Bifrost (say Biv'-rost) (p. 10, 34)
The rainbow bridge that links Asgard to Midgard.

Firth (p. 33, 34, 36)
A narrow strip of water.

Fjord (say fyord) (p. 5, 12, 23, 34)
A deep sea inlet with mountainous sides, like those along the coast of Norway.

Freya (say Fray'-ah) (p. 17-20)
Vanir goddess of love, beauty and war, who goes to Asgard disguised as Gullweig.

Frigga (say Frig'-ah) (p. 34-38, 42-43)
Odin's wife.

Garth (p. 11, 46)
A word meaning "yard" or "small field."

Giants (p. 4, 16-18, 20-33, 41, 45-46)
An evil race of huge beings that menace humans. Many of them are "frost giants" and are covered in frost. They are also called "trolls" and "ogres."

Ginnungagap (p. 6)
Yawning Gap; the emptiness between Muspell and Niflheim, before anything else came into being.

Gjallarhorn (say Gee-all'-ar-horn) (p. 15, 16, 45)
The horn of the watchman-god Heimdall. It can be heard all through the worlds, and will sound the doom of the gods at Ragnarok.

Hel (p. 35, 42-43)
Daughter of Loki, a half-alive, half-dead monster who rules Hel (the same name), the kingdom of the dead.

Hoder (say Hode'-er) (p. 40-41, 46)
The blind brother of Balder.

Ifing (say Eye'-fing) (p. 10, 23)
The river at the edge of Asgard.

Jotunheim (say Yott'-un-haym) (p. 10, 15, 17, 21, 23, 26, 32-33, 37, 42-43)
The land of the giants.

Loki (say Loke'-ee) (p. 21-33, 37-38, 40-46)
Trickster-god.

Midgard (p. 10-11, 14, 16-17, 23, 27, 44-46)
The world of men and women.

Mimir (say Meer'-meer) (p. 14-16, 20)
The wisest being, who has his own well of wisdom.

Mjollnir (say Mee-oll'-neer) (p. 21, 23, 25-26, 32-33, 40, 46)
Thor's hammer, which he uses for many things, especially slaughtering giants.

Muspell (say Moos'-pell) (p. 6)
A realm of fire, to the south of Ginnungagap at the beginning of time.

Niflheim (say Niv'-ul-haym) (p. 6, 34-35, 37, 42)
The world of cold and ice in the north. Hel is in Niflheim.

Niord (say Nyord) (p. 16, 19-20)
The first god of the Vanir, a god of the sea.

Odin (say Oh'-din) (p. 5, 6-16, 18-20, 34-36, 41-44, 46)
The chief god of the Aesir. He is god of poetry, battles, and death. He wears a wide-brimmed hat and a long cloak, has one eye, and often goes in disguise.

Ragnarok (p. 44-46)
The destruction of the gods.

Thor (p. 17-18, 21-33, 40, 46)
The most popular of the Aesir gods, and the son of Odin and Frigga. God of sky, thunder, and fertility. He has a red beard and rides in a chariot pulled by two goats.

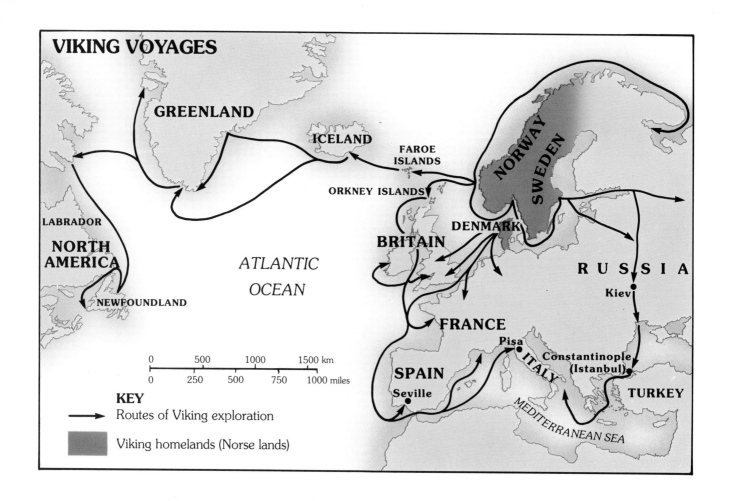

VIKING VOYAGES

GREENLAND

ICELAND

FAROE ISLANDS

ORKNEY ISLANDS

LABRADOR

NORTH AMERICA

NEWFOUNDLAND

ATLANTIC OCEAN

NORWAY

SWEDEN

DENMARK

BRITAIN

RUSSIA

Kiev

FRANCE

Pisa

Constantinople (Istanbul)

SPAIN

Seville

ITALY

TURKEY

MEDITERRANEAN SEA

0   500   1000   1500 km
0   250   500   750   1000 miles

KEY

→ Routes of Viking exploration

Viking homelands (Norse lands)

Utgard (p. 26-27, 32-33)
The fortress of the giants inside Jotunheim.

Utgard-Loki (p. 27, 30-33)
The ruler of Utgard, and a great enchanter and wizard.

Vanir (say Van'-eer) (p. 15-20)
A race of gods, thought of as being earlier gods than the Aesir.

Yggdrasil (say Eeg'-draz-ill) (p. 10, 12, 14, 17, 21, 45-46)
The Tree of All the Worlds, it shelters all the worlds. It has three roots; one in Asgard, one in Midgard, and one in Niflheim.

Ymir (say Eem'-eer) (p. 7-10)
The first giant, and founder of the evil race of giants.

Further Reading

Branston, Brian. *Gods and Heroes from Viking Mythology.* New York: Peter Bedrick Books, 1993.

Daly, Kathleen N. *Norse Mythology A to Z.* New York: Facts-on-File, 1990.

Green, Richard L. *Myths of the Norsemen.* New York: Viking Children's Books, 1970.

Hamilton, Edith. *Mythology.* New York: Little, Brown & Co., 1942.

Hook, Jason. *The Vikings.* Look Into the Past. New York: Thomson Learning, 1993.

Norse Myths and Legends. Tulsa, OK: EDC Publishing, 1986.